S0-BRJ-460

*Creatures of the Wild*

# Buffalo

General Editor:
Ann Mallard
Department of Biology, City College of San Francisco

Photography by
Alan and Sandy Carey

CHARTWELL BOOKS, INC.

This edition first published in 1998 by
PRC Publishing Ltd.
Kiln House,
210 New Kings Road,
London SW6 4NZ



CHARTWELL BOOKS INC.
A division of BOOK SALES, INC
114 Northfield Avenue
Edison, New Jersey 08837

This edition was produced by American Graphic Systems, Inc., in cooperation with the
Northwest Natural History Society (NWNHS)

Designed and captioned by Bill Yenne



We are grateful for the information provided for this book by the US Fish & Wildlife Service

*Notes on terminology:*
The North American buffalo is properly referred to as a "bison," although "bison" and "buffalo" are used interchangeably, and the latter is more common in regions of the United States where the species is present. For this reason, we have used the term "buffalo" in this book.
According to the United States Endangered Species Act, the term "endangered" means a species is considered in danger of extinction throughout all or a significant portion of its range, while "threatened" is a less dire category, meaning a species is considered likely to become endangered, but not in danger of extinction.



ISBN 0 78580 8302

Printed and bound in China

# Buffalo

General Editor:

Ann Mallard

Department of Biology, City College of San Francisco

The North American buffalo (*Bison bison*) is the largest land animal in North America. While a moose stands taller at the shoulders, a buffalo is longer and weighs more. Certainly, the buffalo was the most numerous large mammal ever to exist in North America. It is believed that the ancestors of the buffalo crossed over a land bridge that once connected the Asian and North American continents during one of the Pleistocene ice ages, between 200,000 and 800,000 years ago. These ancient bison were enormous compared to the modern day animals. Skulls have been found on the Great Plains with huge curving horns up to six feet across (compared with a spread of 35 inches today).

During the Ice Age these great beasts died out and were replaced by smaller forms. Some of these had flat horns like those of the water buffalo of India, and some had short horns like the present animal. The North American buffalo, *Bison bison*, was the main survivor of this evolution. Through the centuries the buffalo slowly moved southward, retaining their heavy fur covering, and when the Europeans discovered America, the huge herds had spread throughout North America, along the Atlantic coast to Florida and south into Mexico. Especially on the Great Plains, from the Rocky Mountains east to the Mississippi River and from Great Slave Lake in Canada to Texas, they prospered until the animals numbered in the millions.

The North American buffalo is properly referred to as a "bison," and there is an ongoing controversy over the use of the term "buffalo." This term probably had its origin with the naturalist Mark Catesby, who referred to the animal as a buffalo in his book *The Natural History of Carolina*, which was published in 1710. Today, the two terms, "bison" and "buffalo" are used interchangeably, and the latter is more common in regions of the United States where the species is present. As J. Walker McSpadden wrote in 1917, "Early settlers called it the 'buffalo,' and it has been a buffalo to Americans ever since." However, the National Bison Association prefers the term "bison," and "bison" is now the more commonly-used word in Canada.

The North American buffalo belongs to the family Bovidae, as do domestic cattle. The North American buffalo is closely related to the European bison, or wisent (*Bison bonasus*), and the Canadian wood buffalo, but only distantly related to the "true" buffalo species of Africa and Asia. These include the cape buffalo (*Syncerus caffer*) of Africa and the various water buffalo, which range from the Philippines to Egypt.

The cape buffalo was once widely distributed in the southern part of the African continent, but, like the North American buffalo, it is now largely restricted to parks and game preserves. While the cape buffalo is a wild animal, the water buffalo types are largely domesticated. The water buffalo are also the most populous of buffalo species. There are an estimated 25 million in China, and nearly 85 million in India. They are increasing in population in all areas except Southeast Asia. There are two general types of water buffalo, the river water buffalo (*Bubalus bubalus*), which is found from India to Egypt and as far north as Europe, and the smaller swamp buffalo (*Bubalus carabanesis*), which is common to the Philippines and eastern Asia, but is also found in India.

The North American buffalo is a very impressive animal. The huge head and great hump, which are covered with dark brown, wooly hair, contrast sharply with the relatively small hips. The male buffalo, called a bull, often weighs 2,000 pounds or more and stands five to six feet high at the shoulders. Buffalo have a huge hump of muscle at the shoulder which is needed to sup-

*Opposite:* Buffalo have endured harsh weather on the Great Plains for centuries.

port the massive head, and which is much larger in the male. The females, which are called cows, are not as massive, weighing 800 to 1,100 pounds and standing about five feet at the shoulders. The buffalo's heavy coat ranges in color from tan to dark brown, and it insulates them both from the blazing heat of summer and the intense cold of the winters on the Great Plains. The fur is much thicker on their heads and in the heavy cape of fur over their shoulders, which may be protective during battle.

Like their close relatives, domestic cattle and domestic sheep, buffalo have cloven hooves. Both males and females have a single set of hollow, curved horns. Buffalo horns are sometimes 22 inches in length, with a circumference of 16 inches at the base, and a spread of 35 inches from tip to tip. In yearlings, the horns are four to six inches long. Until four years old, the young males are called "spike-bulls." Their horns are jet black. In the adult, they become grayish.

### BUFFALO WEIGHT COMPARISONS

(Adult males measured in pounds, kilograms in parentheses)

| | |
|---|---|
| **NORTH AMERICA** | |
| North American buffalo/bison (*Bison bison*) | 2,000(900) |
| Wood buffalo/woodland bison (*Bison bison athabascae*) | 2,200(1,000) |
| **EUROPE** | |
| European bison, or wisent (*Bison bonasus*) | 2,200(1,000) |
| **AFRICA** | |
| Cape buffalo (*Syncerus caffer*) | 1,540(700) |
| **ASIA** | |
| Water buffalo (*Bubalus bubalus*) | 2,200(1,000) |
| Swamp buffalo (*Bubalus carabanesis*) | 1,320(600) |

*Opposite:* There are far more buffalo today than there were at the beginning of the twentieth century. At that time, a herd the size of the one pictured here would have represented a sizable percentage of all buffalo then living.

Although the buffalo's size and color may vary in different areas of the country, experts generally agree that all North American buffalo belong to the same species. The differences in appearance probably result from the variety of environments in which they live. For instance the mountain buffalo are somewhat smaller than the plains buffalo. However, the wood buffalo, or woodland bison (*Bison bison athabascae*) is now considered to be a subspecies of the plains buffalo. The wood buffalo is larger and darker than the North American, or plains, buffalo, with longer, more slender, horns. Found formerly in the wooded uplands of eastern Canada from Great Slave Lake south, probably to the United States, it dwindled in number in the early twentieth century to a handful of survivors along the Great Slave River. Because of its northern distribution, it was once believed that this animal did not come into contact with Europeans, other than a few trappers, until relatively late in the nineteenth century. The wood buffalo is thought to be descended from a species that once inhabited the mountains of the West but today, this subspecies of *Bison bison* is found almost exclusively in Alberta's 11 million acre Wood Buffalo National Park. The largest national park in North America,

Wood Buffalo was established in 1922 to preserve not only the subspecies, but its unique habitat as well.

Despite their great size and bulkiness, buffalo have amazing mobility, speed, and agility. They are able to sprint at speeds of up to 30 miles per hour. Although they are huge and stocky, buffalo can wheel and charge quickly. Their bones have been found with those of mountain sheep on mountain summits where horses could not find a footing and which man could reach only by climbing. Buffalo are good swimmers and will often cross a lake or river merely to graze on the other side. They swim with the nose, forehead, and hump above water. The tip of the tail, with its bunch of hairs, is held high. In stormy weather, the herd stops and the hardy animals stand or lie facing into the wind. Buffalo appear to have more highly developed senses of smell and hearing than sight. When unable to depend on smell or hearing, they stand and stare.

*Opposite:* A buffalo cow and her calf crossing a shallow stream. Born a uniform buckskin color, such as is seen here, the calves are considerably lighter than the adults. They will darken to brown and black within their first year.

### BUFFALO HEIGHT COMPARISONS

(Adult males measured in inches at shoulders, centimeters in parentheses)

| | |
|---|---|
| **NORTH AMERICA** | |
| North American buffalo/bison (*Bison bison*) | 65(160) |
| Wood buffalo/woodland bison (*Bison bison athabascae*) | 72(180) |
| **EUROPE** | |
| European bison, or wisent (*Bison bonasus*) | 72(180) |
| **AFRICA** | |
| Cape buffalo (*Syncerus caffer*) | 60(150) |
| **ASIA** | |
| Water buffalo (*Bubalus bubalus*) | 72(180) |
| Swamp buffalo (*Bubalus carabanesi*) | 48(120) |

The grasslands of the Great Plains evolved along with the grazers. Buffalo grass was an important food of the wild buffalo herds. This is one of the native bunch grasses which once covered the central part of North America from Mexico to Montana, giving the land a park-like appearance. Bunch grasses tolerate severe winters, long dry spells, and the trampling of great herds, so long as they are not over-grazed (as sometimes happens with cattle). Bunch grasses grow in clumps, and the large crown shades and protects the root area during the heat and drought of summer. They are perennial grasses. The leaves die back during the freezing cold and blizzards of winter on the Great Plains, but the roots remain viable and sprout quickly in the spring. Because the growing point is at the base of the stem they continue to grow even after they have been grazed. These grasses disappeared from extensive areas soon after the last wild herds were destroyed.

With the disappearance of the buffalo, the taller grasses, formerly reduced by the heavy grazing pressure of the great herds, began to reappear.

Introduced species of annual grasses from Europe have also become common. Today on the government refuges in both Canada and the United States, the buffalo feed largely on buffalo grass, bluegrass, bluestems, wheatgrass, and fescues, in combination with other broad leaved plants called forbs, which are more commonly known as wildflowers. When snow covers the range, the buffalo root through the snow with their muzzles and heads, unlike horses and cows, which paw through the snow with their hooves first.

Because the great herds were nearly gone before any organized attempts were made to survey populations, we may never know just how many buffalo once roamed North America. Estimates, based on the number that could have been sustained by the food available in their natural environment, range from 30 to 75 million. In the nineteenth century, some estimates — including one made by General Philip Sheridan — exceeded a billion. There were so many that early observers resorted to phrases such as "numberless," or "The country was one black robe" or "The Plains were black and appeared as if in motion" with the herds of buffalo. Reports penned by trappers and explorers who travelled into and across the Great Plains in the early nineteenth century frequently describe single herds numbering 3,000 or more. The Lewis and Clark expedition, encountering a herd at South Dakota's White River in 1806, observed, "The moving multitude darkened the whole Plains. We are convinced that 20,000 would be no exaggerated number." Similar descriptions of solid masses of buffalo stretching for "as far as the eye could see" are common.

In 1869, William Street, an Army officer in Kansas, observed a herd that filled an area 20 miles by more than 60 miles square, and moved continuously at one to two miles per hour through a valley for over 24 hours without having passed. Allowing 25 square feet for each animal, the size of this one herd would have easily exceeded one million buffalo.

Perhaps the most amazing account of all is that of Yale paleontologist Othniel Marsh, who was looking for fossils in Western Kansas in 1872. He sighted a particularly large buffalo herd which filled an entire valley, six to eight miles wide and perhaps 12 miles long. In amazement, he spent some

*Opposite:* A Wyoming herd grazing along the Yellowstone River, late in the season, before the first snow.

time trying to estimate their numbers and came up with 100,000 animals. As it was late in the afternoon, he then decided to shoot one for dinner. When he selected his animal and rode downwind into the herd he suddenly realized that he was surrounded, and that the whole huge mass was not only disturbed, but moving and gathering speed. Marsh decided he could only ride out the stampede, trusting in his horse — a fleet Indian pony — and using his gun to keep buffalo on either side from getting too close. It was a nightmarish ride, not just over flat plain, but jumping over gullies, scrambling through canyonlands and avoiding the treacherous holes and tunnels of the prairie dogs. Fortunately, just as his pony was quivering with exhaustion he was saved by a small butte which stood directly in the path of the stampede. There he and his pony sheltered while the huge herd thundered past. It was more than one hour before the last of the buffalo passed them by, and they were free. Such accounts do much to catch the flavor of the days of the great wild herds, but also make one wish that a scientific study of these great herds had been undertaken. It is a pity that no systematic count was attempted when the vast herds were still extant. The first such "buffalo census" was conducted in 1889 by the Smithsonian Institution. By this time, however, there were only 1,091 of the animals to count, fewer than in single herds of a generation before.

Whether from choice or from necessity, vast numbers of buffalo moved northward in the spring, and southward in the fall, and this migration was observed and reported for about a century. As Ernest Thompson Seton wrote: "Theoretically, the buffalo must have been migratory. Although they covered a vast region, they continued [to be] of one species, whereas, they would probably have split up into several distinct species had they not been continually mixed as the result of migrations." Yet the great north-south migrations once ascribed to the buffalo never occurred. The treks probably were not more than 400 miles long, as the herds moved in various directions in their search for food and water, as well as to escape hot weather on the southern Plains. These great herds were actually made up of smaller groups or "sub-herds."

*Opposite:* A buffalo grazing at dawn along the misty Madison River in Montana.

**POPULATION ESTIMATES**

|  |  |
|---|---|
| 1820 | 75,000,000(?)* |
| 1870 | 5,000,000(?)* |
| 1880 | 1,000,000(?)* |
| 1889 | 1,091 |
| 1895 | 800 |
| 1902 | 1,394 |
| 1905 | 1,697 |
| 1910 | 2,108 |
| 1920 | 8,473 |
| 1930 | 19,000 |
| 1950 | 23,000 |
| 1970 | 30,000 |
| 1980 | 65,000 |
| 1990 | 100,000 |
| 1995 | 200,000 |

* For most of the nineteenth century, the buffalo population of North America was considered "limitless," so no effort was made to conduct a systematic count. It is known that the numbers were drastically reduced by 1870, and between 1880 and 1883, the annual kill exceeded 200,000. After 1884, there were too few buffalo to make hunting economically viable.

Only when panicked did these smaller groups appear to lose their identity and merge into the great mass of the large herd. It is unknown whether the original small herds ever reformed after a stampede.

Explorers, hunters and settlers on the Great Plains described many buffalo stampedes as terrifying but spectacular events. A herd of wild buffalo could stampede on the slightest provocation — the howl of a wolf or coyote, the barking of a dog, a flash of lighting, or the sound of thunder. Only one buffalo need be startled and head off at a run for others to join him and set off a chain reaction. Suddenly the peaceful herd could become a surging mass pounding across the land for miles, trampling everything in their path, including the buffalo within the herd too slow to keep up, who would be pounded to death. Descriptions by early settlers caught in the path of such a stampede are harrowing. The herds were so immense that the noise was deafening, and many people said that such a mass could never be stopped or turned aside. However, there are several accounts of small groups of three or four men who were able to part the oncoming herd by shooting steadily into the approaching mass.

In the spring, buffalo begin to shed their heavy winter coats, and soon their hair hangs in tatters. As the bison shed their coats, leaving much of their hind parts naked, they suffer much from the attacks of mosquitoes and from the prickly seeds of the spear grass. The huge animals avail themselves of any convenient boulder or the trunks of trees against which to rub themselves, in their desire to gain relief from their insect scourges. The early telegraph poles over the Plains were frequently knocked down by the buffalo rubbing against them. Buffalo also roll in the mud or dust to scratch themselves or rid themselves of insects. Early travellers on the Plains wrote of the "buffalo wallows," which they they found scattered from Nebraska to Idaho. These dusty depressions were often a foot or more deep and 15 feet across. Today, some of these old buffalo wallows can still be seen on the Plains, their circular outlines marked by the difference in the vegetation growing on them and on the surrounding areas.

With the arrival of the breeding season in July and August, the herds become restless. The bulls, aloof most of the year, now drift among the cows and calves. Noticeably quiet at other times, the bulls bellow hoarsely and become quarrelsome. Many fights occur over females, and the combatants, with lowered heads, paw the earth defiantly. When a bull is angry, his tail is brandished straight up in the air, like a danger flag, and soon he will charge. The fight itself is fast, and horns are the main weapon, aimed at the opponent's head, neck and shoulders. The stomach, however, is the most vulnerable spot, and a good jab in that region will end the battle. The combined bellowing, or "roaring" as it was once called, of the bulls at breeding time can be heard for miles. These battles are always fierce and often bloody, but rarely fatal on the open range. Once it became obvious that one of the contestants was beaten, he would hobble off, and the fight would be over. Fatal fights are

*Opposite:* The buffalo bull may have horns that are nearly two feet long. Headdresses made from the buffalo's head and horns were highly prized by the Native American shamans or "medicine men."

much more likely to occur in small herds of captive buffalo where the loser cannot escape.

During the latter part of the breeding season the animals of all ages and both sexes have intermixed in the herd. After September, the males become indifferent to their partners, and separate themselves into one herd and the females into another. This phenomenon was, curiously enough, noted by the first Europeans to observe the animal in the wild. The first Europeans to actually see the buffalo were probably the members of the expedition led by the Spanish conquistador and explorer Francisco de Coronado, who led the first major European expedition into what is today the American Southwest and Plains in 1542. Coronado and his party reported that they had observed herds of bulls without a single cow, and other herds of cows without bulls.

The cows usually give birth annually to a single buff-colored calf. Most of these calves are born between the middle of April and the end of May, but

*Opposite:* In the nineteenth century, trains crossing the Plains and prairies often had to be halted to allow vast herds to pass. Today, the scene is often repeated in miniature in places such as Yellowstone National Park, where herds still roam, oblivious to vehicles filled with humans.

### CANADA: PUBLIC BUFFALO HERDS

| LOCATION | HERD SIZE | | LOCATION | HERD SIZE | |
|---|---|---|---|---|---|
| | MAX. | MIN. | | MAX. | MIN. |
| Wood Buffalo | | | Chitek Lake, Manitoba | 17 | 17 |
| Wood Buffalo NP, Alberta | 3,000 | 3,000 | Banff NP, Alberta | 15 | |
| Mackenzie Sanctuary, NWT | 2,200 | 2,200 | | | |
| Little Buffalo, Slave River, NWT | 450 | 400 | Plains Buffalo | | |
| Elk Island NP, Alberta | 400 | 300 | Pink Mountain, BC | 700 | 600 |
| Hook Lake, | | | Elk Island NP, Alberta | 500 | 400 |
| Slave River Lowlands, NWT | 250 | 200 | Wabasca/Mikkwa Herd, Alberta | 200 | 50 |
| Waterhen Lake, Manitoba 200 | 200 | | Wentzel Lake, Alberta | 50 | 10 |
| Nisling River, Yukon | 140 | 120 | Riding Mountain NP, Manitoba | 45 | |
| Nahanni Herd, NWT | 80 | 60 | Firebag River, Alberta | 25 | |
| Hay-Zama Bison, Alberta | 40 | | Prince Albert NP, Alberta | 20 | |

some arrive as late as October. Buffalo have a gestation period of about nine months (270-287 days), and the mothers usually produce a single 45-55 pound calf, although twins are occasionally observed. The cows can produce calves well into their 20s at a rate of one per year. At birth, the calves have only a faint suggestion of the hump they will develop later. Buffalo begin grazing (primarily on grasses) while still very young, although some may continue to nurse until they are nearly a year old.

Traditionally, the newborn calves were at the mercy of predators such as coyotes and grey wolves, which were known in the nineteenth century as "buffalo wolves." The cow could successfully defend her offspring, but if the assailants were too numerous she would bellow to the bulls for assistance.

### United States: Public Buffalo Herds (Original Great Plains Habitat)

| Location | Herd Size Max. | Herd Size Min. | Location | Herd Size Max. | Herd Size Min. |
|---|---|---|---|---|---|
| Custer SP, SD | 1,500 | 950 | Finney Game Refuge, KA | 130 | 90 |
| Wichita Mountains NWR, KS (USFWS) | 575 | 480 | Samuel Ordway Memorial Prairie, SD | 125 | 85 |
| Badlands NP, SD (NPS) | 550 | 500 | Cross Ranch Preserve, ND (TNC) | 105 | 75 |
| Fort Niobrara NWR, NE (USFWS) | 530 | 400 | Blue Mounds SP, MN | 65 | 45 |
| Theodore Roosevelt NP, ND (NPS) | 450 | 415 | Hot Springs/Glendo SP, WY | 45 | |
| Niobrara Valley Preserve, NE | 400 | 250 | Sully's Hill NGP, ND | 35 | 30 |
| Wind Cave NP, SD (NPS) | 360 | 300 | (USFWS) | | |
| Fort Robinson SP, NE | 325 | | Wild Cat Hills SP, NE | 10 | |
| Maxwell Game Range, KA | 200 | 150 | Kineslan Herd, KA | 6 | 6 |

### United States: Other Public Herds

| Location | Herd Size Max. | Herd Size Min. | Location | Herd Size Max. | Herd Size Min. |
|---|---|---|---|---|---|
| Yellowstone NP, WY (NPS) | 3,500 | 3,500 | House Rock Ranch, AZ | 130 | |
| Antelope Island SP, UT | 750 | 550 | Conner River Herd, AK | 120 | |
| National Bison Range, MT (USFWS) | 475 | 370 | Raymond Ranch Herd, AZ | 110 | |
| Delta Junction, AK | 450 | | Land Between the Lakes, KY (USTVA) | 87 | 60 |
| Henry Mountains Herd, UT | 400 | | Chitina Herd, AK | 70 | |
| Farewell Herd, AK | 275 | | Hot Springs/Glendo SP, WY | 45 | |
| Arizona Game & Fish Department, AZ | 250 | 200 | Sandhill Wildlife Area, WI | 35 | 30 |
| National Elk Refuge, WY (USFWS) | 220 | 173 | Golden Gate Park, CA | 13 | |
| (Grand Teton NP) | | | Pittsburg Herd, AZ | 6 | 6 |
| Fermilab (DOE) | 135 | 55 | Three Islands SP, ID | 5 | |

*Above:* Framed against the backdrop of the rugged Mission Mountains, this big bull is a resident of the National Bison Range in Montana, which was established in 1908 as part of the effort to save and restore the species.

The males would quickly respond and would stand in a circle around the calf, while the wolves circled. After a few minutes, the knot would break up, and, still keeping in a compact mass, would start on a trot for the main herd. In less than a week from their birth the calves are strong enough to run with the herd, and their safety is then assured.

Calves, as well as weak and old buffalo, fell victim to wolves, but far a worse enemy were the prairie fires, quicksand, and treacherous ice on the rivers which, taken together, were responsible for the deaths of enormous numbers of buffalo. Ice on the rivers took a greater toll of buffalo than any other natural factor. Rotten ice on all the northern rivers, totalling in length about 20,000 miles, must have caused the deaths of enormous numbers of

buffalo. In 1807 Henry noted: "The number of buffalo lying along the beach and on the banks passes all imagination. They form one continuous line and emit a horrible stench. I am informed that every spring it is about the same." John McDonnell, in his journal, wrote: "Observing a good many carcasses of buffalo in the river and along the banks, I was taken up the whole day in counting them, and, to my surprise, found I had numbered when we put up at night, 7,360 drowned and mired along the river and in it."

A further natural enemy of the buffalo were blizzards. Ernest Thompson Seton observed in the 1870s that "The great herds that went north in 1870-1871 never returned. There is no evidence that any large numbers of them were killed by hunters, red or white, and there is, therefore, but one reasonable explanation of their disappearance. They were exterminated by the blizzards of 1872. Further, I believe that, of all times, the Dakota blizzard has taken a heavier toll of the buffalo than even the Dakota Indian did."

*Above:* A buffalo herd on the move in the National Bison Range. This herd is descended from the animals saved in the 1890s by Montana ranchers Michael Pablo and Charles Allard and a Native American of the Pend d'Oreille tribe named Walking Coyote.

*Above:* The herd heads toward a stand of aspen. Buffalo will feed in a forest such as this, but, like domestic cattle, they actually prefer to graze in the open.

*Above:* As seen here, the courtship ritual between buffalo involves the bull sniffing, or "scenting," the female whom he wishes to turn into a mate.

## BUFFALO AND NATIVE AMERICANS

The buffalo was a principal resource of the Plains Indians, furnishing them with food, hides for robes, skins for shelter and boats, bones for tools and utensils, and "buffalo chips" (dung) for fuel. It has been said that Native Americans used every part of the buffalo for something. While this is true, research has shown that they didn't use all of every animal they killed. However, there was clearly a sustainable yield. The enormous buffalo population would have continued to support the much smaller native population indefinitely, had it not been for the use of firearms and the arrival of the white man.

Various parts of the buffalo were favored as food. The tongue was especially prized by both Indians and later by whites. The hump was especially

*Above:* Another important part of the courtship ritual among buffalo, as it is with many species, is the duel between two males over the right to have a specific female as a mate.

favored, and the blood, brains and heart were also eaten. John James Audubon observed that the internal organs were also considered as a delicacy, although certain tribes are recorded to have had special preferences. The Kootenay would eat only the heart, while the Blackfeet refused to eat the liver. Buffalo was usually cooked, but not infrequently, especially just after a kill, it would be eaten raw. Meat that was not eaten within a day or so was preserved by drying it into jerky. It was sliced thin and hung on scaffolds over a fire. Jerky was easier to carry because the drying reduced the meat's weight by 80 percent. Pemmican, a mixture of dried meat, fat and wild berries, was also prepared. It has been suggested that the legendary strength and endurance often attributed to the Native Americans may well be a testament to the extraordinary nutritional value acquired from a diet that depended upon a constant supply of buffalo meat, which is now known to be both high in protein and iron, as well as low in fat and cholesterol.

*Above:* A mother buffalo and her newborn calf. As occurred here, females occasionally give birth while standing, although they will usually lie down.

*Above:* Buffalo calves such as these are born with the instinct and ability to stand and walk, but the first time is always a struggle. If they couldn't walk immediately, they'd be easy prey for predators.

The Native Americans used the buffalo hide for robes, shirts, leggings, dresses, belts, moccasins, caps, and mittens. The leather was also used to make tepees, blankets, medicine cases, trunks, cache-pit covers, tobacco pouches, berry bags (the hide of the unborn calf), cooking vessels and buckets, as well as shields, knife sheaths, horse gear, dog gear, saddle bags, lariats, horse-watering bags, boats, rafts, snowshoes, ball covers and netting for lacrosse equipment. The hides were also useful in making rattles, masks and winding sheets for the dead. Native American clothing was made from the tanned, more workable, skins of the cows; their lodges and shields were made from the thick, tanned hides of the bulls. The hair found its way into clothing, headdress ornaments, home furnishings, tepee ornaments, tools and utensils, and brushes. It was also braided into rope. The tail was used as a fly-whisk or to make a knife sheath. The sinew was used as twine, thread, bowstrings, bow backing and arrowhead wrappings.

*Above:* A somewhat bedraggled newborn calf. Calves weigh 45 to 55 pounds at birth and are developed fully enough to walk on their first day.

*Above:* The calf makes his first tentative steps. Buffalo calves are very similar in appearance to calves of domestic cattle, except that their tails are shorter.

*Above:* A buffalo cow and two calves. These two are almost certainly not siblings, as twins are rare among buffalo and occur in fewer than one in a thousand births.

The buffalo's horns were used to make headdress ornaments, spoons, ladles, cups, powder flasks and ceremonial objects such as masks. The skull was adapted for use as various tools and utensils, and the entire head was worn as a mask. Other bones were used in making clothing and ornaments, as well as for knives, scrapers, hoes (shoulder blades), sewing awls, arrowheads, lance points, sled runners (rib bones) and as counters in gambling games. Hooves were used for various ceremonial objects, such as masks and rattles, as well as to make glue. The bladder was used as a drinking vessel and the rough side of the tongue as a hairbrush. The fat was used to make soap, and the brains and liver were used as tanning agents.

However, the buffalo was not merely a source of food, clothing and supplies. It is understandable that as a major part of their lives were centered around the buffalo herds, they took on a powerful social and religious significance. Young men proved their ability as providers by killing the buffalo of

*Above:* Twin buffalo calves are so rare that the National Bison Range in Montana, which carefully monitors its animals, reported only two sets in a 27-year span.

*Above:* Calves are born in late spring or early summer. As is illustrated here, a late spring snowfall is not uncommon in much of their current range on the northern Plains.

their ladies' choice. Young women exhibited their promise as wives by tanning the hides. The buffalo was an intermediary through which the Indians could contact the Great Spirit and by which the Spirit spoke to his people. The bond between man and beast endured through death, as the dead were wrapped in buffalo skin robes to prepare them for burial.

Before the arrival of the white man, the native people hunted from the ground with bows and arrows by encircling a smaller group separate from the main herd. Buffalo calling was an important ritual among many Indian tribes. At the beginning of the season when the great herds were known to approach their area, the Indians would use various buffalo calling rituals to encourage their coming. It was extremely important for the herds to be near at hand for successful hunting. For one thing, transporting such huge animals over long distances was a monumental problem. It was also much safer to hunt in one's own tribal lands. Hunting in contested areas of land was very dangerous, and

*Above:* Within a few days — if not a few hours — a buffalo calf such as this one can progress from merely being able to stand, to being able to leap logs and windfall brush.

going into territory belonging to a rival or enemy tribe to hunt buffalo was practically suicidal. A buffalo calling dance of the Mandan men was described by George Catlin. Fifteen men, each wearing a huge mask made from an entire buffalo's head, would dance constantly for three days. When one man became exhausted, he would sink to the ground and be ceremonially dragged off as if to be butchered and skinned, and another man would take his place in the dance. Other buffalo calling rites took place in secret, sometimes using special "buffalo stones" and other ritual objects such buffalo hair balls. These balls were formed when the buffalo licked themselves and swallowed the hair. When the hair was brought up, it would sometimes be in a perfect ball, up to two inches across.

It was also common practice to stampede huge herds to their deaths, by driving them over cliffs known as "buffalo jumps." Hunters would station themselves safely at the sides of the cliff to kill the wounded animals. It has

*Above:* This trio of less than day-old buffalo calves are in various states of development. The one in the middle has yet to attempt his first step.

*Above:* The herd instinct is strong among buffalo, and the calves tend to gather around one another to socialize on their first day of life. Soon they will be running with the larger herd.

been noted that many Plains Indians believed it was necessary to kill all of the buffalo, as any survivors could warn other herds of the dangers of the jump. For over 10,000 years, the people of the Plains killed large numbers of buffalo at jump sites across the West. The Head-Smashed-In Buffalo Jump near Fort Macleod, Alberta is among the oldest, largest and best preserved of hundreds of buffalo jump sites across the western plains of North America. The name is derived from a legend in which a young man observing the falling buffalo from under a sandstone ledge, like a person behind a waterfall, became trapped as the pile of dead buffalo mounted and he died of suffocation. When people butchering the animals found him, his skull had been crushed by the weight of the buffalo. Another important site is the Madison Buffalo Jump State Historic Site near Three Forks and Bozeman, Montana.

After the arrival of the white man, the Indians came into possession of horses, and later, guns. These permitted the killing of larger numbers of buffa-

*Above:* A buffalo calf nurses from a somewhat impassive mother. Buffalo milk is similar to that of domestic cattle, though it is richer in butter fat.

*Above:* In the case of a twin birth, a buffalo cow may choose to nurse only one calf. Domestic cattle have on occasion been used to nurse abandoned buffalo calves.

lo and an increased standard of living for the Indians. The practice of this sort of "hunting" also led to a less complete use of the full buffalo.

The buffalo also figured in the legends of the Plains people, and each tribe had an elaborate mythology surrounding the buffalo. Of particular importance was the extremely rare white buffalo. The Cheyenne relate the story of the first white buffalo seen by scouts of the tribe. They had just sighted a herd of several thousand buffalo in a wide valley, and among them was a white buffalo, a cow, lying peacefully in the center of the herd. The scouts gazed in wonder as the herd rose and began moving off across the valley, but none of the buffalo moved very close to the white cow. They gave her plenty of room, as if they had great respect for her. From that time on the Cheyenne came to worship the rare white buffalo, which was seen as having "good medicine." Even 1,000 white buffalo out of a population numbered in the millions would be rare, but there are confirmed accounts of fewer than 1,000. In the

*Above:* This coyote will attempt to trick the calf away from its mother's protection. While coyotes are more scavengers than predators, young and inexperienced buffalo calves make tempting prey for them.

*Above:* Unless they are injured, adult buffalo, such as these, have little to fear from a single coyote. Their hooves and horns are potent defensive weapons.

twentieth century, fewer than a dozen have been recorded. Although totally white buffalo were rare, pied buffalo, with white faces and white patches overall, were quite common among the wild herds.

The white buffalo was generally seen to represent the female power of the Earth, similar to the notion of Gaia, or Mother Earth. According to legend, the Great Spirit brought the pipe to the people. She came as a young woman wearing a white buckskin dress and moccasins. After the Great Spirit presented the pipe to the people and explained the significance of that pipe, she left the tepee as a white buffalo calf. In most cases, only a respected chief or shaman would possess a white buffalo robe, for even in death, the white buffalo was powerful. The great Cheyenne chief Roman Nose had a magnificent pure white robe, which he called his "Great Medicine." With the arrival of the white man, white robes commanded a price a hundred times greater than a conventional robe.

*Above:* Coyotes, such as are seen here, will harass a herd and will attack and kill only very young, very old, or crippled buffalo. However, they will scavenge any carrion that has been killed and abandoned by a wolf or bear.

*Above:* Always an opportunist, the coyote quietly investigates a buffalo herd for a vulnerable target. Extremely cold weather, especially when combined with deep snow, can compromise the buffalo's agility, and hence its ability to defend himself.

The most well-known and observed white buffalo was Big Medicine, born in 1933 at the National Bison Range in Montana. He had blue eyes and a knot of brown hair between his horns, but otherwise his fur was completely white. Big Medicine was usually kept in an exhibition pasture, where he was viewed by thousands of tourists. In 1937 he sired a pink-eyed pure albino calf who was blind, but otherwise healthy, and for a time there was talk of using him to breed more white buffalo, but it was decided that this was not the policy of the refuge. In 1943, when the exhibition pasture was being reseeded, Big Medicine was allowed to roam the range during the rutting season. When placed into the general herd, the 2000-pound bull fought his way to dominance over the entire herd. He maintained his leadership for several years. In fact he so jealously protected his harem that no one could approach him. Thus he confirmed the Native American belief that white buffalo were the natural rulers within the herd. In 1947, however he lost his leadership to a

*Above:* A dispute over territory may occasionally result in interspecies rivalry. Here a buffalo lowers his head to do battle with an elk in Yellowstone National Park.

*Above:* Fights with predators and other species notwithstanding, most battles involving a buffalo are with other buffalo. Battle scars such as these usually result from mating, rather than territorial, concerns.

nine-year-old bull named Yellowstone and spent the rest of his life in the exhibition pasture until he died in 1959.

In August 1995, the birth of a white buffalo calf near Janesville, Wisconsin was hailed by Native American tribal elders and spiritual leaders as a symbol of a time of unity among all people, or as a powerful omen foretelling a need for unity, peace and healing. However, the calf's fur turned dark as it grew older. A Lakota Sioux medicine man in South Dakota explained that this change was not inconsistent with the ceremonial legend of the White Buffalo Calf Woman. While buffalo are still an important element in Native American spiritual life, it has been more than a century since they were a practical part of the Indians' daily life. For centuries, buffalo had also fed and clothed Native Americans, but the introduction of firearms and the ravenous non-Indian appetite for hides would upset the balance forever between 1870 and 1890. Since buffalo were once so vast in number, it would have been hard

*Above:* As seen here, young buffalo calves will stick quite close to their mothers at first, especially while nursing, or when the grass they are learning to graze is suddenly covered in a spring snowfall.

*Above:* This excellent view shows important differences in appearance between the narrower-faced cow (*foreground*) and the larger and stockier bull.

to imagine that they could have been pushed to the precipice of extinction within a generation, but they were. Their recovery was due to the efforts of foresighted conservationists who recognized the problem just barely in time to do something about it.

*Above:* In observing the herds today, it is hard to imagine what the Plains were like when they were "black with buffalo." Did the big animals stand in tightly packed clumps, as they were often described, or did they move in somewhat dispersed groups, as seen here?

## FROM THE BRINK OF EXTINCTION

By about 1800, the small buffalo herds that had existed east of the Mississippi River were gone. The last buffalo was seen in Pennsylvania in 1801. Buffalo may have been killed to protect livestock and farmlands in that region, and they were probably hunted for meat.

With westward expansion of the American frontier, systematic reduction of the Plains herds began around 1830, when buffalo hunting became the chief

*Above:* A group of buffalo brave a ground blizzard in Wyoming. During the long, bitter cold, high Plains winters, some of the buffalo will freeze to death — as they always have.

Above: While they are remarkably sure-footed, and good swimmers, these buffalo are taking the path of least resistance.

industry on the Plains. Organized groups of hunters shot buffalo for hides and meat, often killing up to 250 buffalo a day. In 1850, 100,000 buffalo robes reached St. Louis en route to the East. In the spring of 1854, Sir George Gore made a hunting trip into Montana that netted 2,000 buffalo. The construction of the railroads across the Plains in the middle years of the nineteenth century further hastened the depletion of buffalo populations.

The most notorious of buffalo hunters was William F. "Buffalo Bill" Cody. Though he is best remembered for his Wild West Show, Cody literally made a name for himself as a buffalo hunter. In 1867, he was hired by the Goddard Brothers, who had a contract to supply meat for construction crews on the Kansas Pacific division of the Union Pacific Railroad. In just 18 months, Cody supplied 4,280 animals. This total would, however, be exceeded by many other hunters. It was Cody's flair for self promotion that placed his name in the history of the great animal that became his namesake.

*Above:* As seen here, herds of buffalo will occasionally use man-made highway bridges to cross rivers and streams in Yellowstone National Park and throughout the West.

*Above:* Unlike their cousins on the previous pages, this buffalo herd crosses a stream in the same way its ancestors did when they migrated from Asia in the Pleistocene.

After the transcontinental railroad lines were completed, it became remarkably easy to ship buffalo hides and buffalo meat to the East. Based on railroad shipping records and other data, 3,158,730 buffalo were killed by whites, and 405,000 by Indians in Kansas alone between 1872 and 1874. The hides sold for an average of two dollars each, but it was still good business. During the winter of 1872-73, the peak season for hide shipments, one firm reported handling 200,000 hides, more than 1,600 pounds of meat and $2.5 million worth of bones. Buffalo bones were shipped to Eastern cities, where they were ground up for use as phosphorous fertilizer or bone char. After the early 1870s, when refrigerator cars became available, it was possible to ship buffalo meat to the East year-round.

But buffalo were not only slaughtered for money. There were so many buffalo and the country was so huge and so new that no one could imagine the killing could do any harm. Thus they were often slaughtered needlessly.

*Above:* Throughout their first summer, calves such as these tend to stay close to their mothers' sides, to nurse, to feel safe and to learn about the world they'll soon inhabit as adults.

*Above:* Buffalo on the move. It was once thought that buffalo migrated over great distances. In fact, the great herds probably never ranged farther than a radius of a few hundred miles.

Hunting from train windows was advertised widely, and passengers shot them as the buffalo raced beside the trains. People came from Europe, as well as from the eastern United States, purely for the sport. The irony was that these animals were hardly dangerous, and so large that little skill was needed to fell one with a bullet from a gun.

Perhaps even more unfortunately, many people at the time — including some of those in the United States government, such as Secretary of the Interior Columbus Delano — also wanted to eradicate buffalo as a way to take away the livelihood and well-being of Native Americans. Native American tribes depended on the buffalo's meat and hides, and many still today believe the animal has special spiritual and healing powers, making it an important part of their culture.

As the Kansas herds were depleted, the hunters moved north into Montana and Dakota Territory. In 1882, about 200,000 hides went east from this

*Above:* With a powerful lunge, this cow hurls her half-ton body onto the bank of the stream. The calves, which are about a fifth of her weight, will scamper ashore.

area by rail, but only two years later, the last carload left Dakota Territory because there were now too few left to make commercial hunting viable.

Conservation of the buffalo came slowly. Idaho had passed regulations governing buffalo hunting in 1864, and Montana and Wyoming followed suit in 1870-1871. Yellowstone National Park, created in 1872, was the first place where killing buffalo was totally banned. With the ban enforced by cavalry troops, Yellowstone had the single largest concentration of buffalo by 1884. With the formidable herds gone, predators also took their toll.
Poachers infiltrated Yellowstone Park, and a census 1894 found only 20 live buffalo. Congress then rushed to pass the National Park Protective Act, which increased the fines and even threatened imprisonment for buffalo poaching.

Unprotected buffalo had no chance; they were still being killed by Westerners — both white and Native American — for subsistence.

*Above:* The intention in creating this herd in Yellowstone was to preserve the species as a microcosm of the herds that existed prior to the nineteenth century.

*Above:* The North American bison is unlike any European species currently extant. Early Spanish explorers compared buffalo with camels (because of the texture of their hides), and with Spanish or Moroccan bulls (because of their temperament).

*Above:* A calf leads the way as the herd breaks into a run.

*Opposite:* Unlike horses, who paw through the snow to get to the grass, the buffalo will push his nose through the snow until he finds grass, "rooting" like a pig.

Finally, in 1897, four buffalo, probably the last free ranging unprotected herd in the country, were exterminated. As noted earlier, the population estimate made by the Smithsonian Institution in 1889 showed only 1,091 buffalo — down from 75 million in 60 years. Other estimates show that there were fewer than 1,000 left by the 1890s. The US Fish & Wildlife Service estimates that there were fewer than 300 wild buffalo remaining in the United States at the turn of the century.

The 250 wild buffalo left in Canada were placed under the protection of the Royal Canadian Mounted Police in 1893. By 1922, with rigid protection, the wood buffalo herd had increased to 1,500 animals. Need for additional range led to the establishment of Wood Buffalo National Park in 1922. A herd of 3,000 to 3,500 now ranges this immense area of boreal forest, muskeg, and grassy plains.

*Above:* A pair of older buffalo calves in action, leaping across a stream. By the end of summer, these, and those seen opposite, are no longer tan, but nearly as dark as they will be as adults.

In the United States, the herds held in private hands were an essential part of species recovery in the early years of the twentieth century. Some of the better-known private herds were Charles Goodnight's famous herd in Texas, the Pablo-Allard herd in Montana, and the Blue Mountain Forest Association herd of New Hampshire. It is largely from these three herds that the buffalo on United States government refuges and parks have come.

Michael Pablo and Charles Allard are especially important in the history of buffalo species recovery. In 1873, as the herds on the Plains were being killed in large numbers, a Native American of the Pend d'Oreille tribe named Walking Coyote obtained several calves from the Blackfeet and brought them to Montana's Flathead Valley on the western side of the Rocky Mountains. In 1884, he sold a small herd to Pablo and Allard, who were ranchers in the area. The two took it upon themselves to expand their herd, predicting that there would eventually be a market for the meat of domestic buffalo. By 1895,

*Above:* This photograph is a reminder that the great naturalist George Bird Grinnell once observed that "Cows are much more watchful than bulls. They are always the first to detect danger and to move away from it."

*Above:* Now witnessed in only a few states and provinces in the West, this scene was once common from the Carolinas to Quebec.

when Allard died, the herd numbered 300. In 1904, with the species having been virtually exterminated from its natural habitat, the federal government appropriated money to purchase 21 buffalo from private herds to build up the Yellowstone National Park herd.

Two years later, Michael Pablo offered to sell his herd to the government, but he was rebuffed and sold them to the Canadian government, who used them as the nucleus of a reserve in Alberta. Meanwhile, Allard's widow sold his share to the wealthy Kalispell, Montana banker, Charles Conrad, who made them available to the United States government. These animals would then become the nucleus of the herd that still roams the National Bison Range near Pablo, Montana.

In 1886, zoologist William T. Hornaday needed specimens of the Plains buffalo for the National Museum in Washington, DC. He knew that the Plains buffalo were becoming scarce, but in eight weeks' time, he collected

*Above:* Though this photograph was taken on a tributary of the Yellowstone, not the Ohio, we are reminded that the presence of buffalo encouraged early settlement in the Ohio River drainage.

only 25 buffalo in Montana, an area that had supported tens of thousands just a few years earlier. His thorough search demonstrated that the species was indeed in danger of imminent extinction. Later, in his position as head of the New York Zoological Park, Hornaday continued to work for the conservation of the buffalo. In 1905, the American Bison Society was formed, with Hornaday as president and Theodore Roosevelt as honorary president. Roosevelt persuaded Congress to establish preserves, and, with the help of a cadre of private buffalo owners, the society was able to stock a number of preserves and parks. Ranchers and breeders, finally recognizing the economic potential of the animal, expanded their efforts to preserve and reestablish the buffalo. The buffalo was finally pulled back from the abyss in about 1910, as the census topped 2,000 and continued to rise slowly.

A 1929 inventory counted 3,385 buffalo and, although the count was not precise, it was encouraging enough that the society discontinued its pro-

*Above:* The buffalo rolls, or "wallows," in mud or dust to scratch itself or to rid itself of annoying and biting insects. The great painter and ethnographer George Catlin noted that the buffalo "throws himself flat upon his side, and then, forcing himself violently around with his horns, his feet and huge hump, he plows up the ground still more, thus enlarging the pool till he at length becomes nearly immersed."

*Above:* Some buffalo wallows — depressions in the ground up to 15 feet across — can still be seen on the Plains more than a century after their last use. Others continue to be used today.

grams and activities in 1930. By 1951, there were 12,158, and by 1989, there were 98,000. In 1995, the US Fish & Wildlife Service estimated that there were over 200,000 buffalo in the United States, with about 88 percent of them in private herds. Of the public herds, the federal government manages approximately 6,000, and tribal authorities at least 5,000. The Yellowstone herd is the largest federal herd, and numbers about 3,500 animals. Buffalo also inhabit several other important federal preserves such as the National Bison Range in the Flathead Valley of Montana, the Wichita Mountains National Wildlife Refuge in Oklahoma and the Fort Niobrara National Wildlife Refuge in Nebraska. The three largest private herds are those owned by the Houck family of Pierre, South Dakota, Turner Enterprises and Durham Ranches. Most of the private buffalo owners are members of the National Bison Association, which was formed by the consolidation of the National Buffalo Association and the American Bison Association in January 1995.

*Above:* The mountain buffalo, thought to be a now-extinct subspecies of *Bison bison,* was observed in what is now Yellowstone National Park from 1806, when John Colter first explored the area. The animals in the present Yellowstone herd, seen here, are theorized to a hybrid of the mountain and plains subspecies.

*Above:* A picturesque view of buffalo in Yellowstone National Park. The Yellowstone herd is now stabilized at roughly 3,500 head, which have their run of the park's two million acres.

*Above:* Where the Plains meet the Rockies. This photograph, taken on a Wyoming autumn day, represents a scene that is as it would have existed two centuries ago.

The commercialization and privatization of buffalo herds has played a major role in increasing their numbers.

Bison ranching is a fast growing industry. Bison are bred for their meat and also for their fur. Buffalo meat is today considered a healthful alternative to beef and is widely available in the states of the the Mountain West and also by mail order, even through the Internet. Recent research has demonstrated that buffalo is a highly nutritious food higher in protein, and lower in fat, cholesterol and calories than other meats, such as beef and pork. Recent comparisons with beef cattle also show that buffalo meat has a greater concentration of iron, as well as other essential nutrients. The meat is considered to be very rich in flavor.

Ironically, after a century of restoration, buffalo in many government herds have become so plentiful that government agencies have had to take measures — such as issuing hunting permits — to control the size of the

*Above:* A cow and bull pose calmly. The autumn mating season leads to a gestation period of just over nine months, and to a new generation of calves that will be born in the spring.

herds. Yellowstone now has more buffalo than its winter range can support, and the animals must leave the park to find food. Outside the park, buffalo habitat is also prime cattle ranching land, and as buffalo herds have grown larger, controversy has grown. Should buffalo or cattle have primary rights to graze on public lands? What is more important, animal rights or property rights? Even states rights is an issue — should the federal government or the state government have the final say? All of these conflicting missions underlie the highly publicized Bison kill of the winter of 1996-1997,
when a sizable proportion of the Yellowstone herd was destroyed in a controversial attempt to protect the Montana cattle industry from the disease Brucellosis.

Brucellosis is an infectious disease which causes buffalo, elk and beef cattle to abort their calves, although most infected buffalo are able to bear live calves after the first abortion. Ironically, it was first introduced into North

*Above:* A pair of buffalo on a hillside in Yellowstone National Park. By October or November, when the snow comes to stay, these animals must be prepared for the winter.

*Above:* The buffalo must be able to root through the snow to get forage. The deeper the snow, the harder the winter will be for the buffalo herd.

America through infected European cattle. The disease spreads easily among buffalo within one herd because they they congregate during calving. Other buffalo groom the cow or calf and may lick the aborted fetus or placenta, which is the primary way in which the disease is transmitted. However, there has been no proven transmission of the bacteria which cause brucellosis between buffalo herds and cattle.

The cattle industry of Montana jealously guards its Brucellosis-free status, which was granted by the US Department of Agriculture Animal-Plant Health Inspection Service (APHIS). Brucellosis-free status enables the livestock industry to ship animals interstate without having to test them, a process that the cattle producers say would cost them between $15 and $20 million per year. APHIS stated that Montana ranchers could lose their brucellosis-free status if their cattle were infected from the buffalo herds. As the Yellowstone herds grew larger, more animals left the park during the winter to

*Above:* A dead buffalo, or one that is merely napping.

*Above:* The sun breaks through the clouds to shine upon a big buffalo bull rooting through a blanket of newly-fallen snow, looking for something to eat.

*Above:* The snow is shallow enough for these buffalo to easily find something to eat. Too deep a snowfall would make the digging difficult, but relatively thin ice would make it impossible.

find food, and ranchers feared that their cattle may be contaminated by brucellosis, which is carried by about 50 percent of the Yellowstone herd. In 1995, after controlled hunts in Montana and Wyoming during the late 1980s and 1990s, in 1995, a suit was brought against the Park Service and other agencies by the state of Montana. A settlement agreement stipulated that most bison migrating toward the park's northern and western borders would be killed to preserve the Montana cattle industry's brucellosis-free status.

This agreement was in place when the winter of 1996 gathered force as the coldest in over 50 years. By late December, the snowfall measured twice the annual average. As a result, most of the Yellowstone herd began to move down to find food at lower elevations outside the park. Ironically, the exodus was facilitated by well-groomed trails kept open for snowmobiles. As the animals moved out of the park they were shot by sate and federal

*Above:* In 1844, near what is now Laramie, Wyoming, a huge buffalo herd met disaster when a heavy snow thawed and refroze. Unable to dig through thick ice, they perished. An ocean of buffalo bones remained there as a landmark for a quarter century.

personnel acting in compliance with the management plan.

As the buffalo body reached 1,000 by April, many environmentalists expressed concern. Even Yellowstone Park superintendent Mike Finley commented that "when people describe what's happening here as a national tragedy, I don't disagree with them. We are participating in something that is totally unpalatable to the American people, and it's something we are not convinced that science justifies."

Native Americans also entered the debate. The InterTribal Bison Cooperative (ITBC), headquartered in Rapid City, South Dakota is an organization of 40 Native American Tribes from 17 states which is dedicated to the restoration of buffalo populations on tribal lands in a manner compatible with the spiritual and cultural beliefs of Native Americans. The ITBC, in cooperation with the National Wildlife Federation, recommended that buffalo leaving Yellowstone should be safely captured and tested for brucellosis, and those

*Above:* Getting enough to eat is only part of the struggle for survival for buffalo such as these in the winter. When temperatures drop well below freezing, the herd must huddle together for warmth.

*Above:* There is safety in numbers when the herd huddles together during a freezing blizzard, but the animals at the center of the huddle will be safer than those on the perimeter.

testing negative should be transferred to tribal lands. Those testing positive should be placed in a research program aimed at creating an effective brucellosis vaccine (the current one is only 65 percent effective). It was also suggested that Yellowstone should try to acquire additional winter range land and key migration routes by purchasing private lands to the north and west.

Meanwhile Jim Knight, a wildlife biologist at Montana State University Extension, had outlined a plan for the elimination of brucellosis from the Yellowstone herd. He advocated trapping, testing and eliminating the diseased animals. Even if this reduced the present herd by 50 percent the population would remain a viable size of about 1,000 and the over-crowding on the current range would be relieved. This procedure had already been tested in a smaller herd at Wind Cave National Park in South Dakota. "They expected to have to repeat the process for three winters," said Knight, "but at the end of two years, park personnel could find no more brucellosis-infected bison."

*Above:* When the deep snows come, the buffalo is vulnerable not only to cold and hunger, but to wolves. A herd can circle itself to defend against a wolf pack, but a lone bull will have a harder time.

*Opposite:* This proud bull will survive the winter, and his species will survive indefinitely. Historically, the greatest threat to the buffalo was neither weather nor animal predators, but rather a widely accepted belief by humans that their numbers were infinite and that they could be hunted without caution forever.

*Above:* Magnificent creatures in a magnificent wilderness. The rescue from extinction of the buffalo in the early twentieth century was the first major effort in the history of planned species recovery.

The controversy over bison brucellosis demonstrated the difficult balancing act that must be maintained by federal and state agencies whose mandates are to maintain a healthy environment for both wildlife and domestic livestock. While the livelihood of ranchers must be protected, the the preservation of a viable herd in Yellowstone is also essential. Indeed, the events of one terrible winter underscored the buffalo's importance.

This great beast is a symbol that is integral to the cultural history of the North American Great Plains. While the buffalo's image no longer graces the American five cent coin, it does appear on the official seal or flag of the states of Kansas, Indiana and Wyoming and the province of Manitoba. It is also used in the insignia of the Royal Canadian Mounted Police, and the official crest of the US National Park Service includes an image of the white buffalo.

Yet this magnificent animal is not only an important part of a past historical legacy, it is part of North America's cultural and environmental heritage, and it must continue to thrive on its traditional range.

*Above:* A buffalo bull grazes quietly on the shore of Yellowstone Lake. Since 1884, the largest protected wild herd of buffalo in North America has lived in Yellowstone National Park.

*Above and opposite:* The image of the buffalo is an important symbol for Native Americans, and for non-Indians as well. It appears on the official seal or flag of four states or provinces and is used in numerous insignia and logos throughout the United States and Canada. This provides a constant reminder that this magnificent animal is not only an important part of a past historical legacy, but a constant part of our North American heritage.

# INDEX